French Quarter Cantos

A Poelage

Genaro Jesse Pérez

French Quarter Cantos
A Poelage

iUniverse books may be ordered through booksellers or by contacting:

iUniverse
1663 Liberty Drive
Bloomington, IN 47403
www.iuniverse.com
844-349-9409

ISBN: 978-1-4502-7777-8 (sc)
ISBN: 978-1-4502-7778-5 (e)

Print information available on the last page.

iUniverse rev. date: 03/18/2021

Contents

To the Patriarch
Teniente de Navío
José Vicente Llinás López

Decapolis

Come and see
Eyes who hear me,
Ears who see me.
Who do you say that I am?
All that is dark will not
Be revealed!
I am possessed by a demon lover
And serve a powerless,
Myopic god
Who will not make you
Shine like the sun
Nor raise you up
On eagles' wings,
For he does not hear
The cries of the poor.
Come and see
A false prophet wandering
The narrow streets
Of this old town
Wearing a tattered coat and a soiled hat,
Begging for quarters
To quench his thirst.
Hunger has many names.
When revelation appears
And the veil disappears,
A child will whimper:
Armageddon is here.
Deception is now
The bastion of modern life.

To a Lady Without Pity

(To John Keats)

I met her along Iberville Street,
Rosy flesh and hair so red, like
Cardinal feathers that flew about
As she ran down the Quarter street
With light feet and eyes wild blue.
She looked at me and asked me to follow
To her slave quarters on Royal Street
She could not wait to taste her sugar cube
And needed a sitter to guide her through
The many dreams she hoped to envision.
When she melted the cube on her tongue
And I kissed her lips,
I felt her darting
Between my teeth like
A velvet minion swan,
The mythical third nipple
Infusing sweet venom.
Sweetness that gave me visions,
Fantasies from keen erotic trances
I had never endured:
I dashed through the streets of a Quarter
So dark and so empty, with a moon so pale
That only death could call it its own.
The early morning storm
Awakened me at the damp riverbank
With a sky crowded with diamonds
Cold, wet, and afraid,
And I never saw again
That beautiful girl sans mercy.
Loitering through the Quarter streets,

Night after empty night,
I search for her in thrall
Whenever I glimpse
A face so fair
With rosy flesh and a red head of hair.

Rejections

Rejections come and go.
Age multiplies them
Like snowy hairs,
Piling high like forgotten dreams
Among layers of memory,
Fading oh ... so ... slowly into oblivion
Until the next one materializes.
The horror of them is
Awakening like dogs
Barking at alley cats.
Perhaps I don't have
The gift of tongues
And divine madness
Vital for acceptance
Here, there, and everywhere.
It all eludes me.
Words collide meaninglessly,
Buried in a lexis cemetery.
Would that I could conceive
Elegant conceits,
Shiny metaphors,
A fragrant kaleidoscope
Of the senses, and perchance,
Too young and not meek,
Gentle yet not tamed,
They could parade like shadows.
Frequently curious,
With rosy lips and cheeks,
They covet with hungry eyes.
Yet, like cautious birds,

Like editors of little magazines,
Uncertain of merit and cost
Oh … how long is the night
That never finds a day!

Upon Writing the Great American Novel

There he was.
Janos in his pad,
In the Quarter
Between puffs of grass
And debauched nights,
He was writing it.
Better than Faulkner's,
Superior to Hemingway's,
And more erotic than Henry Miller's.
Those were his salad days,
When sleep began at daybreak,
And the nights were counted with words,
And often erotolalia brightened darkness
Like lightning streaking
Across a thunderous sky.
Mad music slipping
Through the cracks
In the window panes,
Scraping gray matter.
It is so misty and gray
For a youth to make his way
To fame and fortune, unknown.
Through his old age he became
An old man left in the rain,
Without readers.

Dirty Old Man Mississippi

Obscenely slouched by the Quarter's banks,
Boats and barges massage its crooked
back that hunches about like a pregnant
rat on the litter-infested rocky banks.
Raw verdure is strewn about the levee.
Blinding spring's yellow sun rebukes me.
Albatross with lurching gait, limp and weak,
Fly, you must, in elegant circles above them
Whose dirty, sinuous secrets
They whisper each to each,
Revealing intestines
Blue and bright,
With unwholesome reverie.
They speak of mystic ailments
And Botero's paintings,
As the rust of age quiets them
Onto death's trance.
An old man reeking of stale lust
Snakes about these ancient banks.
Dare I ask—dare I ask
The question on your lips:
Do I wear a mask?

Falls Return

(To Coleridge)

It is a rainy and fallish day.
The wind whistles through
The chimney's pipes,
Making music my cat understands.
The fire from the logs pirouettes,
And I tremble convulsively.
Will I merit fifteen minutes,
Wailing still for my demon lovers?
Fama and Fortuna, a charming duo,
Flee from me, and no longer
With gentle foot stalk my quarters.
I dream of the sunny dome of pleasure
On Saint Ann Street
Where the damsel with the dulcimer sang.
I fed on cherry pies and jelly rolls
And drank the Emperor's tea.
I shall meet them each, one by one.

Fame

You are so renowned.
Everyone knows your face,
Yet no one knows your name,
And you don't know
Everyone knows you
As you walk up the stairs
Of the subway station
Where the celebrated
Photographer took your photo.
Yet, it did not matter.
It did not matter, after all,
As he slowly continued his ascent
Into the street and home
To his wife and children,
Fading into an anonymous life.
Fame is not a plant
That grows on mortal soil.

I Find No Peace

(To Sir Thomas Wyatt, the Elder)

I find no peace, for I must go on
Through jagged academic seas.
Scylla and Charybdis await,
Beastly beauty on one side,
Whirlpools of protocols on the other.
Treachery is often sweetly done.
Desert lovers are unwelcome.
Flying above the wind
Burdens me with ire.
I can see the glowing fire
Where the vilest worms dwell.
A cloud of dark disdain
Greets my verses.
There are too many friendly foes
With double faces.
Smack! Music seeps
through the windows,
gnawing at my brain
as Giant Despair enters the room
to justify the ways of men.

Dried Voices

(To T.S. Eliot)

His dirty fingers torment
An old broken lyre
while his hoarse voice
sings of salad days.
The placard on the floor
exhorts pedestrians
to drop coins in his tin cup:
"I am testing for human kindness."
Wearing a rat's coat
And sullied feet,
His body exudes
A stale cadaver's stench
And seems venereally tainted.
I can sense the murmur,
The murmur of maternal lamentations.
Unredeemable time awaits concessions.
How can I bear so much reality?

Desk Jockey

(To Hart Crane)

I never dreamt of becoming
A desk jockey.
I wanted to travel,
Become a physician
Without frontiers for
All my assigned years,
Comfort people in misery.
I was born too early, though,
In a place far away.
My cinnamon skin didn't help,
For legal affirmations
With no relevant affiliations
Before societal revolutions
Tried to level the playing field,
To some people's dismay.
But it does not matter, after all,
Not anymore at all,
For I became a hero
To my weeping daughter
Very late one December night:
Two large and furious Dobermans,
Children of Erebus incarnate,
Roaring and growling hell's wrath,
Wheezing wreaths of steam,
Pinned her petrified calico kitten,
Flattened with fear,
Under a merciful car.
It was a sinister and wintry night
When I, shoeless, rushed out,
My dear Louisville Slugger

At the ready in my right hand,
Gingerly stepped on the leprous lawn
And rescued her calico cat.
Snowflakes drumming on my hair,
Chill rippling down my neck,
I could count the strokes of my pulse.
I must make meek adjustments
And be contented
With random consolations.

Blue Boy

(To Marianne Moore and Charles Baudelaire)

He sleeps his time away without scruples.
Winters are made for hibernation,
As are all the other seasons.
From time to time he forays
To his jungle in the backyard:
An emperor surveying his domain.
Woe to those helpless fledglings
So prematurely ejected
From their familiar nest,
Their strewn feathers display
An early and bloody mortality.
He speaks in tongues hard to decipher,
Regulating them to his whims and wants:
A baritone intonation when hunger strikes,
An intense wailing for backyarding.
The tenor surfaces at night,
With melancholic gusto and might,
As he remembers those salad days
When the alleys were his realm,
Before the vet's knife ended
Woe, oh so soon, his sexual bliss.
That Thomashood he proudly exhibited
During his promiscuous tomcatting verve
When he serenaded his sweethearts
Under the glow of many moons.
Before day breaks he jumps on my bed,
Demanding breakfast without delay
With my toes between his paws,
His mystic pastel blue eyes
Become alien and sinister in the dark.

Petum lucidum makes him strange.
His age and weight keeps him caged,
No longer supple enough to soar
Over high walls and picket fences.
Slumbering is most essential now,
Adorning the living room furniture:
A white Siamese with yellow points
Like a great sphinx lounging about.

Piquant Birds

(To Edwin Muir)

They fly about carefree
And take a few seeds from me.
I can't cuddle and enjoy them.
They're forbidden to touch,
No matter how much
They demand to be clutched.
Woe to me and my reverie,
Beset by evil thoughts.
There is always a room
And a bed, perhaps of roses.
They and I lie there
With sinful thoughts,
Fastened mouth to mouth
And breast to breast.
Have I sinned, oh God,
In deathless innocence,
Their scents on my bed
The stains on the sheets?
Woe is me, I can scarcely breathe,
Often fearing societal indictments,
That mark of shame made manifest.
Angry shadows fight on the walls.
Am I a robber seeking lusty bodies?

Dolores

(To John Betjeman)

She is so near and yet so far.
To desire her is to face their ire.
Her red hair and golden skin,
Her plump lips shaped for sin:
Oh, to drink that goddess's potion.
I am left winded, weak, docile,
Her captive slave, willingly bound
With flaming ropes of cherished hair.
Yet my White Goddess is not aware
Of my late-flowering lust unbounded.

A Poem a Day

(To Charles Tomlinson)

They arrive unexpectedly,
Like a gaggle of geese in October,
Pirouetting in a cloudy sky.
Does quality trump quantity
Or vice versa?
Is a great painting
Forgotten in an attic
A work of art?
Is an unread solitary poem
Poetry, or a buried unknown?
Should I leave you alone
To grieve your own meaning?
Let us go together hand in hand
And discover what it is you want.
Does a poem a day
Keep the psychiatrist away?

Cyclops

(To D. H. Lawrence)

Decades have briskly turned
Like the soiled leaves
Of a well-written book.
We used to talk about
Cyclops in *Lady Chatterley's Lover*,
Your face upturned to mine,
Your pastel blue eyes
Distilling the pleasure only I
Could give you. You whispered
Repeatedly, like prayer
During a midnight Mass.
You weren't a young country lass
Even then when you explained,
Between those happy tears,
That I was Juan in a million.

Mississippis Slow Flow

(To T. S. Eliot)

Moving without pressure
Along the crowded banks,
Winding along toward the gulf,
Sweating diesel and oil,
The scars from barges and ships.
Black and brown fouled water
Carries the smell of decades
Of toil and sorrow.
There is no hope for a better tomorrow.
The treachery of men is so sweetly done.
Old Man River's run will not last long.

Just a Little Kiss

(To Mozart and Ezra Pound)

If you gave me a little kiss,
I would coo coo with bliss.
I have grown weary
Of harlots cheaper than hotels.
Here am I, a man with no fortune,
With no name nor mane to come.
It is not precisely the fashion
To stimulate a durable passion.
You, White Goddess, have posed
For decades at the Tate Museum,
Your blazing hair burning the frame
Of your portrait and your golden flesh,
That touch-pleasing antique porcelain,
Glittering like the lubricious treasures
From *One Thousand and One Nights*.
Smitten with passion, I grieve
For very soon, too soon, I must leave.

I Am Nobody

(To Emily Dickinson)

I walk the streets of the Quarter,
Searching for an epiphany
That will inspire me into the creation of
A great poem or story, the great novel.
Up Royal Street and down Bourbon,
Where the tourists move about
Like busy ants gathering food,
Drunks stagger and shout.
Trumpets and saxophones blare
As old strippers cater their wares.
A jazz funeral makes the scene,
The brass band blaring dirges.
There are no saints, only sinners,
And I joyfully join the second line.
Everyone here knows what it means:
Are you second-lining too?
I must cut my body loose,
Tell my name to an admiring Bog.
How very common and ordinary is
The wish to be extraordinary.

Comic Book Hero

(To Blackhawk)

I sat alone and lonely
In a bar gloomy and sullied by time.
"The Good Friend's Bar" is
Frequented by Quarter-dwellers:
Pimps, trulls, addicts, and queens.
Its cheap beer and white lightning
Bury life's torments speedily.
This evening, like many others, it is
As indistinct as the shells on the floor.
Then something happened
for one to muse over:
A masked man came in wearing
A nylon stocking over his hairless head.
Holding a pistol silverish and petite,
He spoke softly to the bartender,
A man telling his friend a sad story.
An unctuous demeanor notwithstanding,
The gun was on the forehead of his quarry.
I was alone at a table behind him
The handful of regulars sat on stools.
The scene became cinematically slow
As a light in my head started to glow.
I clutched my Dixie beer by the neck
And smashed it onto the robber's skull.
As I rushed out to the street I heard
Screams and shouts and furniture falling.
I was also stunned to discover
My tattered T-shirt had now on its front,

In a circle, the head of Blackhawk.
Night swallowed me down Royal Street.
Traffic, tourists, and bars hailed me
With that proverbial French Quarter beat.

Sweet Love of Youth

(To Emily Brontë and Rubén Darío)

Youth is so soon gone and forgotten,
A treasure lost without reflection,
Yesterday's flowers in the dustbin of time.
Those days of golden dreams
Are only perished recollections.
Memory's rapturous pain
Gives me little satisfaction.
Behold the musings of an old man
Sentimentally longing for empty cups
That will no longer be refilled to satiation.

I Had a Dream Last Night

(To Dylan Thomas)

I woke up morose and depressed.
Although the dream I had forgotten,
A mist of old friend and lovers remained.
I was prince of the French Quarter.
The old streets had trails of daisies,
And I was green and carefree.
Everybody knew my name:
"Jesse James, oh, Jesse James,
Won't you write a poem for me?"

Lemmings

(To Robert Herrick and Psalm 23)

They prefer to remain mute rather
Than engage in any dispute.
All those new rules, regulations
That will eventually be a damnation:
Grad students banging into *parietes*
With "preferred minorities" out cold.
I preach—*so alone*—righteousness
For his name's sake, as I was told.
I have lost many dainty mistresses by
Articulating the ramifications of decisions
Erupting from false prophets' visions.
Do I dare; do I dare to turn back
And not leave it all behind,
Like yesterday's friends entwined,
Posing in other times between other places?

Lets Make the Sun Run

(To Andrew Marvell)

What do I hear at my back?
The barking of the dogs very near.
I should curl into a ball with fear.
Yet, as in the past, I shall overcome.
Do not dismiss my crescive faculties.
The afternoon has gone away,
But the evening summons with promises.
The rains will return for yearly rites.
I am ready to use fire in my attack,
And clarity will reign once again.

Angels

(for García Lorca)

On a pin's head,
It is said,
An infinite number of angels spin.
Would I split the atom
If I were to explain it all
Once and for all:
Much better than yesterday,
not as well as tomorrow?
The murmur of the mass
Cocoons our embrace
As refrains of refrains
Are doled out like alms
At the entrance of churches.
I felt your golden breasts
Open to me suddenly and blossom
Like precious, ripe fruits
Through our winter garments.
I am still titillated
After all these years
At such recollections.
How many have we known?
You were once
Naked on that hanging terrace.
It's now long ago.
When you danced for me,
Your hardened and red nipples
Resented the morning's chill
Descending over Carmona.

Weeping Woman

(To Tino Villanueva)

I could hear her moaning
In my bedroom
During those windy and wild
West Texas nights.
Often a thousand violins
Began to play tunelessly
As I awaited, unhappily, another day,
My back in pain from the *pizca*.
A bale a day is not enough.
Where are they now
After all these years?
Are words truly the answer?

Divine Madness

(To García Lorca)

Oh, sacred lunacy, inspire me.
Allow me to describe your light.
One thousand and one angels reflect
Your wisdom and love.
Grant me speech,
One thousand tongues
To describe your greatness.
How should I presume to portray
Her elusive body dancing nude
In the moonlit plaza
Without your inspiration?

Certain Contribution

(Romans 15:26)

Is it too much to ask
To be allowed
A certain contribution
No matter how minute, like
Threads of protoplasm?
Would that I could
Be written in/into space.
But I thrust myself into this maze,
This mazed world of words,
All torment, trouble, wonder, beauty.
Oh! To have greatness thrust upon me.

Life is But a Span

(To Shakespeare's Othello)

Outsport indiscretion, she claimed.
The newspaper eagerly reported.
She showed the videographers
The jagged scar crossing
Her upper left cheek.
How could she be so meek,
Some asked, gallionic wonderers.
Her husband was cleansing his honor by
Drawing blood from her cheek.
She now wonders about her casual lover.
Where could he possibly be?
And her husband is on the lam.
Life is complicated by decree.

Prepare a Face

(To T.S. Eliot and Abe Lincoln)

I do not have the ability
To describe others
As they see themselves:
Am tactless to a fault
And have no spare faces
That induce cordial embraces.
I wear my independence
Like an old tweed suit.
I am a stranger in an arid,
Strange, academic land.

A Furtive Tear

(To Donizetti)

It appeared at the corner of her eye,
Slid down her left cheek
Like a downhill ski champ
On the rosy flesh that I worshiped.
Her turquoise eyes were
Flooded with anguish,
Drowning in despair
As she supplicated for answers.
"She is yours;
I never did offend you in my life."
Her hair on fire, as the morning
Sun was reflected in her red strands:
Perjured woman stoning my heart!

Award for Long Service

(To John Betjeman)

The decades danced by,
Leaving behind the taste
Of many Saturdays
And the proverbial Mondays.
I presumed much and expected more.
How does one explain how
Decades come and go
Like the shifting seasons?
The plaque came and went.
The speeches and greetings
Left very little to remember.
I cling to life, inflamed with fear,
Remembering the joys I knew
When I was young in sin.

Elpida

(To Robert Graves)

Drunk with excitement
At your impending visit,
I remember your dancing eyes
And subtle smile
Promising journeys (re)taken
So very long ago.
And now, almost forgotten,
Memory bleaches old,
Faded black-and-white photos
Without mercy, in fast motion:
An unknown slapstick silent movie.
Now I hope for that shivering glory:
To be fed with apples
And the nectar from your lips.
Oh, to touch that fresh fruit's skin tone.

Face Dancers

(To Frank Herbert and John Berryman)

Smiling faces so cordial and congenial
Appear and disappear with the seasons.
There is nothing I can give you
But curses and disdain
For your bad faith
And inauthentic stand.
Malice is pimples on their faces
Henry is speaking at the usual
Cocktail party where the weather shines.
When the chair speaks, they turn into mimes!

Pulitzer

(To John Berryman)

These songs are not worthy
Of the prize of which so many dream
Each night and every day.
These are mere musings,
Fearful and sweet hobo thoughts.
I dreamt of encounters with myself
And very real people who tangled
Fromage and *frottage*, of course,
Fleeing double and plucking the present,
I shall not shake the mapped world!

Sweet Paranoia

(To John Berryman)

The Death Train sweetly approaches
From south to north,
Promising riches and paradise,
A wonderland of manna and spirits,
And white goddesses with bejeweled eyes.
He smoked the pipe of peace and hoped
For young beauties sitting at his feet.
Throngs of souls rose from the train,
A barbed worm inching along.

Song to the Third Age

(To Walt Whitman)

I celebrate that age when nostril hair
Multiplies like weeds
in abandoned buildings.
My breath exudes crowded scents
From decades of distillations.
All females are as paintings,
Deserving closer examination.
Their scents now trigger allergies.
While I am thirsting for their nectar,
Their moist lips readily offer, yet
Their early experiences could expand
The female's sexual encyclopedia.
How can I presume to be a magician
When they could teach me a trick or two?

Felicitous Fortuity

(To Pablo Neruda)

When you informed me of
Your problems with aulophobia,
I told you about my osmolagnia
Like Napoleon in the field
The night before battle.
You asked me to be utilitarian, useful
With those dancing eyes,
Promising so much and rendering so little.
Veiled sunrays drift through the window,
And the left side of my bed is cold.

Louisiana Rose

(To Johnny Cash)

Where, oh, where are you
My Louisiana Rose?
Gone to unknown regions,
Pursuing your rainbow
So long a-a-gone?
Yet, I can't forget your lips
And their saltine kisses.
The Quarter gave us
Jackson Square, where we slept
And made love for so many weeks:
We had a fresh version of living.
It was a cold December, remember?
But we did not want a house.
We gave each other warmth.
When will indifference come?

Cheating Eyes

(To the Eagles and Chuck Berry)

Angel of the night
so young in my bed,
Not a minute over seventeen,
Little Queenie of my dreams,
I could be your father,
Perhaps your grandfather.
Where do you come from?
Are you a chemical hallucination?
So many meaningless words
With profound images?
Are you the proverbial devil
As well as an angel?
Is this the rapture?
Oooh, your greenish stare
That sexual awareness
Beyond your years.
Should I let you come near?
So many issues to fear.

New Orleans is Drowning

Jewel of the Mississippi,
City of my dreams
Where beautiful women
Are real and very near:
I loved them for so many years.
Water covers the city
Like a shroud that smothers
As bureaucracy muddles about.
Help! Help me, mister,
Throw me some water!

About the Author

Genaro J. Pérez (PhD, Tulane University, 1976) is a professor of Hispanic literature at Texas Tech University. He is the author of numerous articles and papers dealing with Spanish American, Peninsular, and Chicano/Latino literatures. His academic books include *Formalists Elements in the Novels of Juan Goytisolo*; *La novelística de J. Leyva*; *La novela como burla/juego: siete experimentos novelescos de Gonzalo Torrente Ballester*; *La narrativa de Concha Alós: texto, pretexto y contexto*; and *Ortodoxia y heterodoxia de la novela policíaca hispana: Variaciones sobre el género negro*. He has also written two books of poems, *Prosapoemas* and *Spanish Quarter Notes*, and two books of fiction: a novel, *The Memoirs of John Conde*, and a collection of short stories, *French Quarter Tales*. Professor Pérez is the coeditor and publisher of *Monographic Review/Revista monográfica*.

I wish to express my gratitude to my daughter, Nicole Therese Pérez, for the cover art.
—Genaro J. Pérez

Printed in the United States
by Baker & Taylor Publisher Services